The **Quiet Builder**

Janice E. McKinnie

THE QUIET BUILDER

iUniverse books may be ordered through booksellers or by contacting:

iUniverse
1663 Liberty Drive
Bloomington, IN 47403
www.iuniverse.com
844-349-9409

Because of the dynamic nature of the Internet, any web addresses or links contained in this book may have changed since publication and may no longer be valid. The views expressed in this work are solely those of the author and do not necessarily reflect the views of the publisher, and the publisher hereby disclaims any responsibility for them.

Any people depicted in stock imagery provided by Getty Images are models, and such images are being used for illustrative purposes only. Certain stock imagery © Getty Images.

ISBN: 978-1-6632-2324-1 (sc)
ISBN: 978-1-6632-2325-8 (e)

Print information available on the last page.

iUniverse rev. date: 05/27/2021

This book is dedicated
to my first
Mentor and Businesswoman

My Mother
Gloria Barr-McCaster
May 15, 1940 – July 4, 2000

"Thank you for giving me the building blocks of my success."

"Faith…
the largest building block
of them all has carried me through
with so much more to
look forward too!"

Janice E. McKinnie, Author

Contents

Acknowledgements

Thank you, God, for giving my gifts and
talents to use for your glory!
Stephanie and Alex thanks for hanging with your
mom from community meetings, on the road,
Late nights at church, trusting that I would take
care of you both with everything I had.

To my husband Sean, I always say God knew
exactly what I needed and when I was
prepared to receive it. Thank you for believing
in me, pushing me and telling me that
I can do this!

I promise to handle your heart with
care and treasure it with love.
unknown

Foreword

It is an incredible honor to write the Foreword for my dearest Friend, *Janice E. McKinnie*, who has taken the wisdom and knowledge of learned lessons and put them into a format, to not only inspire but encourage the community, as a whole, in her very first book, *"The Quiet Builder"*

Janice, has always been a consummate professional, with great interpersonal and administrative abilities and within all of my years of management, I have yet to meet her equal; in her unique ability to multi-task in getting things done. In the world of *"Development,"* if you want to talk about somebody starting a race ten yards behind; *Janice* did just that and made up the stagger to become one of the most accomplished *Female Developers* in *Upstate New York* and she did it the *old fashion way...* through hard work, relationship building and an unyielding desire to learn. Some would think her success was built from her political connections---but I would say, on the contrary; it was due to her dedication and ingenuity; as limited access to resources never stopped her, as you will see within these upcoming pages, how she just kept on *"building the foundation quietly."*

As a wife, mother, sister, friend, and professional woman, *Janice* has been distinctively called upon from *the beginning* to excel, in every area, (sometimes being paid less and perhaps as a woman, not as well respected within the industry of development), however, she has managed it all; overcoming obstacles, to simply make it happen; which comes as no surprise to me, as I have had the privilege of working side by side with her, as we accomplished even *'Church,'* work that was divinely set before us.

I am thankful to the Lord to have a dear friend, who has been there for me, during my *darkest moments*… in the loss of my beloved daughter *Kayla* and one of my *greatest accomplishments* in receiving my Master's Degree in *Leadership*. Nobody gets anywhere alone. We must have those family and friends, at the front seat in our lives, who not only inspire, but also encourage and push us to levels we never thought were possible. The *'Author,'* aimed early on to do just that…. a *'Trailblazer,'* relinquishing untapped capabilities, in order to reach her highest potential. It would behoove us, to never underestimate, the power of an educated and motivated woman, called by God.

Janice, thank you, my forever friend, for never saying *"you can't"* and for always being there for me. *Congratulations* on your first book written for *'Aspiring Developers'* and sharing your gift with others who dare to take on such a daunting task, but you have shown the way… that *"with God, all things are possible."*

Continued success on your incredible journey!
Rasheed NC Wyatt

Foreword

Janice my journey with your mom started at Greater Refuge Temple of Christ at the back of the old church in 1978 located at 943 Jefferson Ave, Buffalo NY.

We would enter through the front doors of the church and proceed to the prayer rooms behind the pulpit, inside were desks and phones.

Missionary Gloria as she was affectionately called would open in prayer with so much love and excitement, I would pass her calls just to see the enjoyment she received in praying with others. Her eyes and smiles were contagious, those were good days, and days you never wanted to miss. The type of faithfulness your mom showed is so rare, she was a true servant. As they say fruit does not fall far from the tree.

I met Janice is 1996 at True Bethel Baptist Church, located at 491 E. Ferry St., she sang and led songs in the choir while being instrumental working in whatever she could to enhance the ministry. We worked for 15 years in the church office together, accomplishing many systems and procedures too many to name, but are still existing today. We had fun and productive meetings, I became her personal shopper, I would shop for her and she would love everything I bought for her. She proved herself to be devoted, loyal and dedicated to building the kingdom. Her tough demeanor earned her the name the *"warden"* she is a true soldier in God's army. Janice knew how to make it happen and this go-getter attitude still stands today.

Minister Rosetta Swain

I

The Beginning

My first mentor and businesswoman was my mother *Gloria Barr-McCaster,* a skilled beautician, medical secretary, caterer, and a loving mother. My dad was a machinist at J.H. Williams Tools where he worked until he retired. He also drove cab for Broadway Taxi for many years. My mother worked for *Dr. Frank G. Evans & Dr. Lydia T. Wright,* two prominent doctors in the African American community general medicine and pediatrics were their specialties. I spent every Wednesday with my mom at her office; I could not have been more than six years old, but I remember it well and that experience landed me a job in my twenties. My mom raised me to be independent and to believe that "I can do anything with that I put my mind to." My mother reminded me all the time that "*can't* was not a part of my vocabulary.

Growing up in Buffalo, New York, from the *Towne Gardens a predominately black neighborhood* then moving to North Buffalo, a predominately white/Italian neighborhood, proved to be quite the undertaking, as I was the only black girl in my kindergarten class at Buffalo Public School # 81 and we were the only black family on my street. I understood, *at an early age*, the importance of needing to do my best more than others just to be recognized as having the same abilities and talents to succeed. My mom and dad wanted to ensure that I received the best they could give me; and they kept me very grounded, in church and many other family activities, in the process.

I grew up watching my mom serve as secretary, treasurer, Women's Day chair, planning events and activities for over 30 years, in the Church. I remember late nights printing bulletins in the basement of *Walls Memorial AME Zion* on Glenwood Avenue with *Ms. May Smith*. At *that time*, I did not know that the atmosphere I was exposed to was building a foundation of what I was to do in years to come. I attended community events and banquets, at a young age, getting all dressed up in my gowns and patent leather shoes, with tons of curls, thanks to my hairdresser of a mom. I remember those banquets honoring African American community leaders, activist, and business owners. Never in a million years, would I have imagined the impact that coincided with my career path, from these very humble beginnings. I received the Black Achievers Award in 2014, by this same organization, whereas a little girl I watched others being recognized. I am truly humbled and honored.

As I grew up in the *African American Episcopal Zion Church*, I considered it to be my first business school, as I was very active serving as president, secretary and on committees for children, youth, and young adult ministries on local, regional, and national levels. I was still in grammar school; yet traveling the country. Organizing events, writing letters to invite speakers to programs and planning fundraisers were all a part of my job at an early age. I have inserted a letter I literally hand wrote to Rev. Darius Pridgen in 1979 inviting him to be a speaker for our youth revival. Who would ever imagine 50 years later that I would have written many letters for such a prominent Pastor.

July 17, 1979

WALLS MEMORIAL A.M.E. ZION CHURCH

455 GLENWOOD AVENUE • BUFFALO, NEW YORK 14208

Rudolph L. Wells

Greetings in the name of Jesus Christ

Dear Brother Prigdon

The youth & young adult ushers of Walls Memorial are having a program. On September 16, 1979 at 5:00 P.M. We would be very honored if you would be our guest speaker. Our theme is, "Children you are the future". We are looking forward to hear from you. Thanking you in advance.

yours in Christ

Valoria Bruckins
PRESIDENT

Janice McCaster
SECOTARY

please let us know soon as possible by aug 27, 1979

Janice
875-5527

All through high school, I stayed active in church, continued to learn, and grow, participated in local activities such as the *"All High Challenger Review,"* in addition to a local newspaper called the *Challenger News* managed, by Editor *Alnisa Banks*, who gave high school students the chance to write on local youth and community events. I will never forget that experience as it

3

taught me the importance of creating and telling *our own stories*. I thought I would be the first *Black* Barbara Walters; this was before *Oprah Winfrey came on the scene... I would have chosen her first.*

As an active Girl Scout, I had the pleasure of having the best Brownie leader ever, *Mrs. Barbara Pridgen*, Mrs. Pridgen had a son named *Darius*, who because he was an only child, unfortunately for him, had to hang with his mother and all the *Brownie girls* for our activities. Darius and I attended the same church and participated in many activities together. We became close and a sister/brother bond was formed; a friendship that would transcend over 40 years. God was already setting things up for his glory without me even knowing. I attended grammar school with *Rasheed Wyatt* I was close friends with his sisters *Kim and Yvette.* Rasheed began attending, *St. Luke AMEZ Church* and joined the *Zion Community Choir* where Darius and I were both members and that is how our bond was formed: the three of us were *inseparable.* Through high school and college, however, taking different paths in life, we celebrated weddings and births of children; Rasheed and I are the Godparents of Darius' children. Together, we each possessed our own special gifts and talents, going on we would accomplish more than what I could have imagined, however, when God is in control, you just sit back, relax, and receive all he has in store for you.

I attended State University of New York at Buffalo *also known as Buffalo State College,* majoring in Public Communications. I started college wanting a career in broadcasting, but once I realized that you had to literally chase a news story, I knew that was not for me. Public Communications was a new major at the college that was a combination of broadcasting, radio, public relations and public speaking. Once again, God orchestrated

4

a *major* that would give me the skills needed for my future. I graduated from Buffalo State College and landed a state job, for one of our local universities, within their department of medicine. This reminded me of when I was about six years old sitting, at my mom's office where she was a medical secretary. It's funny because it's exactly what I said in my interview and it must have held some weight because I was hired for the position as a medical billing clerk. I worked in that capacity for seven years; learning a lot about the operations of medical billing, so much so that I created a position that allowed me to travel to other sites overseeing offices, maintaining the billing, accounts payable and receivables for the university's department of medicine.

I was blessed, in the interim, to become married, have 2 beautiful daughters, but I felt like there was something else for me to do. It probably didn't help that when I mentioned to one of my co-workers that I wanted to work at a certain HMO, in our hometown, and was told, "*Jan, you will be here with us forever!*" There was nothing wrong with being there forever, *just for* someone else.

II

Where It All Started

I am a witness that it is not about "*what you know... but who you know and whose you are*," GOD's. As I felt that continuous pull to do something different, I had a friend who knew someone that knew of a job, at a local health care company who was hiring for a marketing representative for a new managed care program. My resume was shared and I was offered an interview which I took. This was a company, I prayed to work at, and God presented me with the opportunity. My interview was to give a five-minute presentation based on their program which I read off a brochure a day before my interview. I had not done public speaking in years and my only health care experience was that of medical billing, little did I know, another set up by God equipping me with what I needed to succeed. After interviewing, I was offered the job as a Marketing Representative; nothing I had ever done before but I did have a degree that gave me the skill set to use my public speaking and public relation skills. While at the Department of Medicine I learned a lot by working with interns and for multispecialty doctors in a somewhat complexed structure. A structure that would never be understood if you did not experience it firsthand, as I worked in healthcare for 7 years, I went from being a marketing representative, to becoming a physician recruiter, the same doctors that I managed at the hospital and did medical billing for. No one else understood the structure, BUT ME and that became my territory to recruit new doctors; I spent seven years, at this health care organization, going from a marketing representative to a physician recruiter and running a national vaccine program for local pediatricians to purchase vaccines at a wholesale rate. It was a unique position and I was only the second administrator of this program. I continued to work after leaving the company, until they were able to find a replacement. This was my first consulting job.

In 1996, remember my friend Darius, well, he became the pastor of True Bethel Baptist Church and a few years later I joined. What is so amazing is that I remember attending programs with my mom, at this same church located at 491 E. Ferry Street, Buffalo, NY, God was always guiding my footstep leading me back to places I had been.

In 1999, God led me out of corporate America to the ultimate promotion, building His Kingdom. I became True Bethel Baptist Church's first Church Administrator. Now that I look back over my journey of employment, this does not surprise me. Since the age of 14, I created positions that did not exists but was waiting just for me. I never administered a church, but there was never a question in my mind; that I could not do this, remember my mom told me "can't" was not in my vocabulary and not with doing things that involved God.

Rasheed was not far behind me, he joined True Bethel and took a leadership role and here we were all of us back together again, each of us taking our perspective roles in the kingdom. Only God knew what the future would hold and it all started from the first building block of friendship and faith.

As iron sharpens iron, so a friend sharpens a friend.
Proverbs 27:17 NLT

III

Church Administration

In October of 1999, leaving my lucrative marketing and recruitment career at a local health organization to become Church Administrator, was pivotal in becoming a *Quiet Builder.* True Bethel was a small but strong church with faithful members who kept the church going through several transitions of pastors. Under, Darius's leadership the church purchased an abandoned grocery store from a city auction. There would be several phases of expansion because the church kept growing and enlarging our physical space was necessary. God sent many angels to help us through our various stages, ensuring we had all that we needed to continue to expand the kingdom.

As a Church Administrator, I created systems and processes from scratch, having the insight of what I knew from my upbringing in church, watching my mom and what I learned in all my jobs from organizing, to public relations, marketing and dealing with various people; all of it was going to be useful for what I had to encounter for years to come. So, I believe that the position of Church Administrator was another position created for me but directed by God. I served as Church Administrator for 10 years, I was not one that liked to be in the forefront; I like to make things happen from the background.

The next few years, would be tireless and full of sacrifices, being a young mom and wife; balance was something I had not learned quite well yet. As a woman, in a male dominated society, we are not allowed to show emotion, or appear as though we are unable to manage multiple things. It may be seen as a sign of weakness. My attitude was to be strong, handle it and make it happen. It was building character and a personality that would become useful for future endeavors. I believe that God allows you to experience challenges to make you stronger, but more so for you to have a story that may encourage others.

I believe God gives us many gifts but we must remember to ask him for the wisdom and guidance on how we would use those gifts for His glory. *"Perfect Patty"*, a complex I had created in my own head was way too much pressure to handle. It was with prayer and maturity that I overcame this. You do not have to be perfect but consistent in doing better. As an ultimate multi-tasker, I realized I could not do everything alone, and I didn't like doing everything, that's when great volunteers who understood the mission of our ministry assisted with their gifts to enhance the growth of our church.

I have been given the opportunity to use my gifts to create and build for God's kingdom, solid foundations for others to continue to build upon. We often forget *to whom much is given much is required,* and what we do in life if purposeful is not about us at all. God was setting me up for even greater.

In 2003 True Community Development Corporation, the development arm of True Bethel Baptist Church was created and I became the 1st Executive Director. The church knew that ministry should go beyond the four walls of the sanctuary, clothing and food ministries had existed, however transforming a neighborhood seemed like the next thing to accomplish; but it was not- always at the forefront of our minds and we have never done what we know

now as community development. We had never built any housing, the transformation of an 85,000 square foot former grocery store into a sanctuary was just the start of a great beginning. I did not have an urban development degree, nor did I go to school for construction, but I was equipped by God to put people and things together. You start with a few pieces, creating a foundation that you can continue to add onto; creating something bigger and greater that will stand over time.

I had no intentions or desires to ever write a book, however as I continue to grow and gain knowledge of being a *developer*, people often ask me how, what, where, and the best way for me to share my knowledge is to tell my story where it all began and how I got here. I am still amazed, at what God has allowed me to do on his behalf. It is the nuts and bolts of my journey *(nuts and bolts are all the basic components no matter how big or small, that are part of the essentials) 7esl.com.* I believe all the essentials in my life help me to create a strong building block of faith.

Rasheed and I with members of True Bethel at 907 E. Ferry St.

IV

A Crack in My Foundation

My mother was so loving, she was a foster mother to over a dozen young ladies three of who became my permanent sisters. It was because of my mother's love that they were able to become loving wives, mothers, and grandmothers. This is how powerful my mother's love was which continues to spread through generations and is still flowing through each of us building our own family foundations.

In 2000, my world changed forever. My first mentor/ businesswoman was called to heaven. My mom had health challenges that she did not share with anyone including me. I found out one day as I was visiting her in a hospital where I use to work actually and one of the best renal specialists was in her room. He asked, *'what I was doing there'* and I told the Doctor *that this was my mom*; then he responded, *'I will leave you two alone to talk.'* They were preparing mom to receive a stint in a few weeks and then begin dialysis; this happened right before her 60th birthday. I gave her a party around May 15th which was her actual birthday; (her close friends and family came), it was a beautiful time. I saw some of her guest crying and I then realized my mom had not shared with anyone how ill she really was. .

This was just the type of person she was, some of these friends she spoke to everyday and never complained. That was mom! I used to say there could be a fire and my mon would respond, "*we will get out just fine, let's go.*" On July 4, 2000, *Independence Day*, two months after her party, *she received her crown of independence.*

God thought so much of me that he made sure that I would not feel motherless, or without angels here on earth; that is why he gave me Barbara Pridgen and Monita Laurent. My mom set me up real good, giving me *building blocks of faith*, with a mother's love to ensure that even after she was physically gone, others would be here to assist me as I continue on my journey to faith, love, family and success. These two ladies were predestined to be a part of my life, my mom told Monita to watch over me and my girls and that she did. Through some challenging times in my life she taught me about "*behavior is consistent*" and "*divine intervention*". God prepares you and while all things may not work out like you want, "*all things do work together for the good of them who are called according to his purpose.*" *(Romans 8:12).*

Growing up with women leading and being in charge was not out of the ordinary for me; I experienced firsthand, again beginning in the church, my youth leader, Willie L. McCullough, another woman whom I will not forget; she too was very instrumental in cultivating my leadership and business skills. Traveling with her and taking on responsibilities was a part of being a youth and young adult in the AME Zion church. The trust my mom had in God and with these women was one of my greatest blessings.

Good Sister-Friendships were formed from church, my community, schools, and college; the one area of my *inner strength*. I do not talk to all these ladies daily, but our hearts and minds are forever intertwined. We have been there for each other since our youth days, right on down to the stages of mature womanhood. It is important for women to have a good circle of friends, family, or a mentor that do not know you for your titles, jobs, or what you are able to do for them; but they know you just *for who you have always been*. You can be *vulnerable and strong*, at the same time and no one is threatened, yet they support you, in all your accomplishments, as well as disappointments, even when you do not tell them everything... you know that you are in their thoughts and prayers. They keep you humble and protected and for them I am so grateful for their love and support.

Barb and Me

Mom and Me

Alex, Monita & Stephanie

Willie L. McCullough, Me & a few of my Sister Friends

V

Your Gifts Make Room for You

All my jobs starting from summer youth programs to medical biller, marketing rep and church administrator prepared me for the upcoming chapters of my life as a developer. I always believed I was working for a Fortune 500 Company; that just happened to be a church. We have taken ministry outside the walls of the sanctuary and began to build physical walls that empower, provide security, pride and generational wealth through the creation of housing.

I was doing development before I ever realized that was what I was doing. In my 27 years of development, I have been blessed to do the following:

Sanctuary expansions, townhomes project, senior housing, single family homes, adaptive reuse conversion of a former firehouse, in addition to a commercial national retail franchise and commercial district upgrades for local business owners.

Putting pieces together, being behind the scenes, building blocks one person and one building at a time. The *Quiet Builder*, the behind-the-scenes girl, that is who I am.

All roads led me to this very moment, where I have had the ability to organize architects, engineers, and general contractors to create something beautiful and purposeful for others. I hope that my journey provides you with knowledge to create vision, seek understanding of what is needed in your surrounding community and to empower you to build housing, economic development, and a spirit of hope.

I will share with you what I call the nuts and bolts of creating a Community Development Corporation CDC. My years of affordable housing experience from a faith-based perspective I hope will be helpful to you and your endeavors.

Proverbs 18:16
"A man's gift maketh room for him and bringeth him before great men."

TB Senior Estates & True CDC Board at Grand Opening

Single Family Home & TB Townhomes

True Bethel Church and Dollar General

If God has given you a vision, then begin to work the plan, my Pastor Darius Pridgen has taught me that *"money follows mission"*. This is what I remember when I am doing projects, because funding and resources are not always evident, however if you have been given a mission God will provide you with the resources to do exactly what needs to be done.

That is the building block of FAITH in action!

VII

Quiet Builder

My great community, of Buffalo, NY, captured the essence of who I am in an article in Black WNY 2014, about the journey I have taken, by Will Jones & Jasmine Gonzalez. The Quiet Builder came from this article.

Here are a few excerpts from this article that really bring me to this very moment:

> *"There have been many instances when the works has been enriched around us and no one seemed to ask why or how. True Bethel Baptist Church has angels moving stones and building homes but not too many ask, who? Though Darius Pridgen is the beauty of True Bethel, BWNY considers Janice White the brawn."*

> *"Janice is building more homes than I can build using Lego blocks. I asked, how she stays so humble, "Being blessed, I try not to think about it because at any moment it can all be gone".*

"Stepping out from behind the scenes, Janice cheerfully owns her role as a Developer."

"Though Janice stands by the side of Pastor Pridgen every step of the way she cast her own shadow and it's wearing a crown of its own."

I thank *Pastor Pridgen and the True Bethel Baptist Church congregation*, for entrusting me to transform what we call our "*Campus*," building and creating hope for all those in need of adequate and affordable housing.

All roads, of quietly building, have given me the ability to orchestrate something beautiful and purposeful for others.

In 2014, I founded Developments By JEM, LLC a development and project management consulting firm in Buffalo, NY. I assist organizations and businesses to realize their visions of residential or commercial projects also working with faith-based organizations and churches teaching them the steps to create a successful Community Development Corporation.

This is just the beginning of my life as a developer, mentor and teacher, I remain humble and open to His will for opportunities prepared just for me that will impact the lives of others for many generations.

VIII

Nuts & Bolts of Community Development

So many people ask me?

- **How do you create a CDC?**
- **How do you create a board of directors?**
- **Where does funding come from?**
- **Can church members serve on a CDC board?**

At the beginning of creating our CDC, I read, researched and met persons who were doing the things I wanted to do in our community. One of those people happened to be *Rev. Dr. Fred Lucas*, President /CEO of the Faith Center for Community Development, Inc. who developed senior housing, Head start programs and more, in New York City. He committed to work with me for several months, teaching the basics of community development. One thing I remember, in which I still live by today is... *"he who owns the land owns everything."*

I had the opportunity to meet *Rev. Dr. Floyd Flakes*, founder of the Greater Allen Community Development Corporation and visited some of his projects in New York City. The Greater Allen Community CDC had a focus area in which they created senior, affordable and veterans housing. He shared with me the importance of leveraging to make projects happen, both financially and socially. These experiences helped me to form a *foundation* to begin to *build* our own CDC. I encourage talking to other CDC directors and boards, to find out how they have accomplished what they have, and what were some of the challenges and how did they overcome them. Networking and seeking knowledge from others who have been successful in the areas you are looking to accomplish; I believe is a vital key to success in this business.

Do we really want a CDC and what does it take?

An advisory committee or volunteers may be formed to begin To look at what is needed in your surrounding community to be certain what your mission is and bring to fruition the vision you are looking to accomplish. A CDC's efforts are to enhance and improve the conditions in a targeted or area of focus.

I am often asked if there are government grants that fund the starting of a CDC. Start up grants, or government funding normally requires at least a year in operations or a proven tack record of activities. This also shows, the investment from within and your value to this endeavor.

What is a CDC?

Community Development Corporations (CDCs) are 501(c) (3) non-profit organizations created to support and revitalize communities, especially those that are impoverished or struggling.

CDCs often deal with the development of affordable housing. (https://www.naceda.org/)

When creating a CDC, it is important to remember this is a business and formation thereof is that of a separate entity, federal identification number (FEIN) and bank account.

Filing paperwork varies from state to state; a CDC is not a federal designation and rules differ. It is important to know your state's regulations and seek highly advisable legal advice.

Federal Tax Identification Number - FEIN: is needed when you start any business. A CDC is no different. You will also need this when you open your bank account. Please note, you do not pay to obtain a FEIN # it is a free process through the federal government.

(https://www.irs-ein-tax-id.com/) find a good lawyer and bookkeeper/accountant early on in your formation to assist you in making sure filings are done on a regular basis and that records regardless of how large or small are accounted for.

What is the Role of a CDC

The role of a CDC is to revitalize communities, via assessment and outreach; the best way to do this is to find out what the needs are, what is lacking and hear directly from people. Knowing where the community came from versus where it is presently, is vital. Look at the neighborhood's strength, weakness, opposition, and threats. This can be done through a real exercise with community stakeholders, (residents, churches, business owners, etc.).

- Research history of neighborhood past vs present
- Neighborhood Strength Weaknesses Opposition Threats analysis

- Create focus area with boundaries of where you want to develop.
- **ASK THE COMMUNITY!!!!!**
- Surveys
- City Strategic Plans – what does the city envision for the area

Creating a Board of Directors

Beginning years of formation of a CDC is based on volunteers until you have raised capital to hire staff.

Your board of directors should be representative of various individuals from the community, financial institutions, legal field, housing, or those that have the expertise or skill set that can assist you with your mission and goals. The number can be as less as 5 (five) or as much as 13 (thirteen). You should at least start out with a president, vice-president, secretary and treasurer remember you can do much with little if you have the right people on board.

Many people ask me should our Pastor be on the board or even the board chair; based on my experience, every organization operates differently. However, it is important to keep the duties and responsibilities separate of any church ministries or boards. In my journey, the Clergy assisted with collectively casting vision, while not serving in any formal capacity within the CDC. You will need to have fair representation of church, community, business, legal and even government expertise that serves on your board.

Mission, Goals & By-Laws

The board should create a mission and goals along with by-laws to lay a foundation for the purpose of your organization.

Sample Mission Statement

"YOUR COMPANY NAME HERE" is a human services organization, striving to make a difference in the lives of 'YOUR CITY/STATE HERE" residents. "YOUR COMPANY NAME HERE" mission is to drive community development, providing faith-based leadership, housing, and human services which will serve as a foundation for revitalization and restoration for under-served and under-utilized communities.

The next key to success is to create a strategic plan, or what I call a "*road map*" for your organization to follow. This should help you accomplish your mission and purpose and is important so you do not find yourself *chasing* funding, instead of your mission.

Experts from the National Congress for Community Economic Development (NCCED) say CDCs are "legally the same as any other non-profit entity organized under section 501(c)3 of the Internal Revenue Code." To become a 501(c)3 your organization will have to contact the Internal Revenue Service (IRS) to have an application mailed or you can visit www.irs. gov, select the charities and non-profits link and download Form 1023. Follow the instructions given by the IRS to complete the process. Non-profit status is necessary to apply for various funding including grants and gifts. https://careertrend.com/how-to-form-a-community-development-corporation

Hiring staff or Executive Director

This step may start out as a volunteer or part-time position, for someone who may have the time and expertise. Salary is not a huge factor, however, as time moves on within the first two years, you will need a dedicated full-time employee to handle the duties of the position. The director, is the *face* of the organization and may need to wear multiple hats in the beginning of starting your CDC.

Raising Capital/Fundraising

Most funding received by community development corporations is received through grants and funding from local, state, and federal agencies. A large portion of these dollars are restricted for the project with percentages available for operations and future projects. Excellent record keeping and filing of annual financial reports are necessary to remain in good financial standing.

Local private funding and foundations along with community development block grants are also helpful depending on what your focus is for your CDC. Lastly, annual fundraising is an important piece of keeping your organization functioning and with revenue that is *not* restricted. Funders look to see that you are not only depending on their funds for survival or projects but that you can sustain if their funds are not available.

This is not easy and is where most not-for profits struggle. Sustainability is achievable with consistency and persistence.

Partnerships

Partnerships and collaborations are great resources to transform neighborhoods and build capacity in CDCs. Most of the projects, I have been involved with have been done in partnership because we wanted to be successful and our partners had what we needed to form a solid development team to create a project from beginning to the end. Partnerships allow you to learn and become co-developers on projects sharing in knowledge, experience, risk and financial gain. It has been one of the best building blocks to our success.

Project Creation & Implementation

Your first project should be based on your community needs and assessments. You will need a manageable plan both in finances and capacity to handle every step to successful completion. Here are a few suggestions that I have used and have been successful. This was a snapshot of the tools I see as necessary to begin the formation of a productive CDC.

- Select a development team (architect, general contractor, partner, co-developer
- Pre-development (site control do you own the land)
- Focus Area – where is your project? (street, neighborhood)
- Viability of your project- (cost and market analysis) bank/ funder relationship

Resources and References

http://hud.gov

http://hudusers.gov

http://faithcenter https:/

https://greaterallendc.org/

https://www.developmentsbyjem.com/

https://www.useful-community-development.org/

"It is with hard work ethics and tireless dedication that has allowed, the author, to become a very prominent development consultant figure in Western New York."
– David Pawlik, CSS, Inc.

Printed in the United States
by Baker & Taylor Publisher Services